Veg

Copyright © 2023 Kids & Culture, LLC
Second Edition

Notice of Rights

All rights reserved. No part of this book may be reproduced or transmitted in any form or by any means, electronic, mechanical, photocopying, recording, or otherwise, without the prior written permission of the author. For information regarding permission for reprints and excerpts, contact info@kidsandculture.com.

Notice of Liability

While every precaution has been taken in the preparation of this book, neither the author nor the publisher shall have any liability to any person or entity with respect to any loss or damage caused or alleged to be caused directly or indirectly by the instructions contained in this book.

Books may be purchased by contacting Kids & Culture at:

www.kidsandculture.com

Jania Otey, Executive Editor
Lovenda Burnett, Contributing Editor
Jamia Eaton, Camp Logo
Donette Lowe & Kolade Kolawole, Book Cover Design
Beverli Alford, Interior Design, Layout, and Food Photography
Madea Allen, Organic Soul Chef, and Food Stylist
Tracey Tannenbaum, Indexer

PERSONAL DEDICATION

Without God Almighty and the unwavering support of my husband, Melvin Otey, Kids & Culture Camp would not have survived and thrived for over a decade. Thank you for giving me the space to do what I do best. Thank you for your unconditional love, which has allowed me to create a dynamic program not only for our own children but for thousands of families it has serviced in the Washington, D.C. metro area and beyond. Thank you for your patience and for sharing my vision to create a culturally enhancing program that has helped shape the hearts of our precious children and future world leaders.

ABOUT THE AUTHOR

Jania holds a B.A. in political science and a J.D. from Howard University. She has enjoyed eating a plant-based diet for over 20 years. Her loving husband, Melvin Otey, is a preacher and Professor of Law. Although she is admitted to practice law in Maryland and the District of Columbia, Jania devotes most of her time to educating and shaping the hearts of her two amazing sons, Caleb James and Christian Joseph, being a wife, working in the church, and running Kids & Culture Camp. In her spare time, she enjoys relaxing at home and reading books about health and wellness.

Jania Otey, Esq.
Founder and Executive Director
Kids & Culture Camp

ACKNOWLEDGMENTS

Thank you to all of the past and present teachers, staff, volunteers, parents, and community partners who have helped make Kids & Culture Camp a success!

Directors

Jania Otey, Founder & Executive Director
Majidah Muhammad, Deputy Director of Camp Operations
Jamia Eaton, Deputy Director of Camp Operations & Marketing
Lovenda Burnett, Deputy Director of Pre-Camp Operations
Oluwatoyin Tella, Deputy Director of Camp Operations & Counselors in Training

Jessica Silva, Deputy Director of Education
LaTeisha Williams, Deputy Director of Supplies & Culinary Arts

Special Instructors

Ras Omar Kush, Yoga Instructor
Jennifer Ray, Certified Children's Yoga Instructor
Contra-Mestre Bomba, Martial Arts Instructor
Mahiri-Fadjimba Keita, African Drum Instructor
Baba-C, Storytelling
Princess McDuffie, Arts & Crafts
Anthony Arrington & Israel Felix, Sports & Fitness
Baba Obi Egbuna, African History
Dr. Quito Swan, Vaughn Bennett, & Miriam Forster, Chess

Behind the Scenes

Raphael Evans, Videos and Digital Media
Nereyda Dunn, Administrative Support
Janisha Richardson, Accountant

Additional Instructors

Kahlil M. Kuykendall
Maya Johnson
Preshona Ambrita Ghose
Karen Mitchell
Emunah Ammizahvad
Monica Reynolds

Adirah Aishet-Tsalmiel
Jawana Msola
Aliya Bowie
Vanessa Richardson
Valorae Cole Graham

Jennifer Muhammad
Zimriyah Moses
Wendy Christian
Michelle Glasby-Millington
Mariama Conte

Kids & Culture Camp thanks Organic Soul Chef Dr. Madea Allen, who prepared the featured dishes. Dr. Allen is a professional chef, way-shower, and full-spectrum health facilitator. She teaches families to create real health insurance. In 2005, Dr. Allen founded Organic Soul Chef. OSC aims to heal and empower communities through sustainable lifestyle education and transformational wellness services. She delights taste buds with cuisines heavily influenced by the African Diaspora and the intersection of culinary practices, history, and culture. Her Integrative Medicine practice inspires clients to live and be well. Dr. Allen's vision is to transform family health globally, one kitchen at a time.

KIDS & CULTURE CAMP'S FOUNDING MAMAS

Jania Otey
Kids & Culture Camp (KCC) has been a labor of love since its inception in 2010. In founding KCC, I aimed to instill in our children an enthusiasm and an appreciation for learning about global cultures while providing a safe and nurturing environment.

Jamia Eaton
KCC has been a blessing in so many ways! It has provided a safe environment for my homeschooled children to learn and have a ton of fun. KCC is an asset for developing successful tools in social development and advancement as they mature.

Jessica Silva
We started with a collective goal in mind, and through hard work, determination, and passion, it became a reality that is still going strong!

Oluwatoyin Tella
At KCC, our children witness their mothers organizing and implementing original ideas, thereby laying the groundwork for future leaders and visionaries.

LaTeisha Williams
Giving children meaningful ways to learn about people around the world is an invaluable gift. They discover that our similarities outweigh our differences.

Adirah Aishet-Tsalmiel
KCC gave my family the opportunity to be a part of creating something desirable for our community. I believe in its power to create global thinkers who recognize the existence of a brotherhood and sisterhood that transcends boundaries throughout the world.

Kahlil Kuykendall
We planted the seeds of our collective vision for our children's education, and today, it has blossomed into our own global village.

Zimriyah Moses
Being part of a collective where children learn, express themselves, and explore our world has been a gift.

Jennifer Muhammad
KCC has been a wonderful experience. We return each year because of the instructors who nurture our children and bring excitement to the learning experience!

Sabrina Boyd
KCC gave my children a place to grow in the comfort and confidence of who they were born to be. KCC is the best-kept secret in Washington, D.C.!

Jessica Macauley
I value my children learning foundational facts and developing a fondness and respect for the countries they explore.

Sabrina Boyd, Oluwatoyin Tella, Khalil Kuykendall, Adirah Aishet-Tsalmiel, Jessica Macauley, Jania Otey, Zimriyah Moses, LaTeisha Williams, Jamia Eaton, and Jennifer Muhammad

Jamia Eaton, Jessica Silva, Jania Otey, Adirah Aishet-Tsalmiel, and Oluwatoyin Tella

History of Kids & Culture Camp

Jania Otey, the founder of Kids & Culture Camp, wanted to infuse her children with a love of learning about cultures from around the globe. In 2009, she began researching summer camps and enrichment programs in Washington, D.C., but her research revealed that many of the programs were singular in focus and very expensive. Jania sent an email to the Sankofa Homeschool Community and asked if anyone was interested in starting a camp. The responses were favorable and numerous.

After countless emails, conference calls, and meetings with homeschool moms, Kids & Culture Camp (KCC) was founded in March 2010. This diverse group of multi-talented educators was committed to inspiring children ages 3-12 to love learning, embrace culture, and live mindfully. Since its inception, KCC has offered four weeks of programming each summer, as well as some winter and spring sessions. In 2020, KCC began offering online classes, curricula, and homeschool resources.

Each year, KCC's incredible staff develops weekly lesson plans for the various age groups to guide the children on a cultural journey that includes the exploration of nature, cooking, music, history, foreign languages, geography, art, literature, exercise, science, and math. In 2011, cooking classes were incorporated into KCC's weekly programming. Campers prepare and savor healthy and delicious vegan cuisine from the various countries and regions they study. This cookbook is a compilation of Kids & Culture Camp's journey of cuisines from around the world. *Although many of the dishes are traditionally made with meat, the recipes in this book are suitable for vegan and dairy-free diets.* These dishes have been cherished by campers over the years, and we are confident that you will enjoy them as much as they have!

TABLE OF CONTENTS

THE AMERICAS

Hoppin' John	10
Three Sisters Stew	12
Teepee Cones	14
Canjica	16
Vegetarian Gumbo	18
Doce de Abóbora	20
Wild Rice Cakes	22

CARIBBEAN CUISINE

Rellenos de Papa	24
Banana Festival	26
Patacones	28
Tamarind Balls	30
Tortillas Panameñas	32
Johnny Cakes	34
Vegetarian Trinidadian Pelau	36

ISLANDS OF THE WORLD

Jagacida	38
Salady Voankazo	40
Samosas	42
Batido de Piña	44
Sopa de Plátano de Timbirich	46

AFRICAN FARE

Curried Lentils with Injera	48
Koshari	50
Jollof Rice	52
Ghanaian Spinach Stew	54
Chakalaka	56
Atkilt Wot	58
Derere	60
Nyimo Patties	62
Matooke Katogo	64

ASIA & AUSTRALIA

ANZAC Biscuits	66
Stir-Fried Bok Choy	68
Vegetarian Thai Spring Rolls	70
Banana Pops	72
Sushi Rice Balls	74
Basmati Rice Pilaf with Apricots	76
Vegetarian Mie Goreng	78

KCC AT A GLANCE   81

Index	97
Glossary	100

Unusual ingredients have been noted in italics. Please see the glossary for descriptions.

Hoppin' John
(South Carolina-Gullah)

Hoppin' John was originally a Lowcountry food before spreading to the entire population of the southern United States. Hoppin' John may have evolved from the rice and bean mixtures that nourished enslaved West Africans en route to the Americas. The roots of Hoppin' John have been further traced to similar foods in West Africa, particularly the Senegalese dish Thiebou Niebe. In the Southern U.S., eating Hoppin' John on New Year's Day is thought to bring a prosperous year filled with luck. The peas are symbolic of pennies or coins, and a coin is sometimes added to the pot or left under guests' dinner bowls.

Serves 6-8

Ingredients
- 2 cups dried black-eyed peas
- 1 tablespoon extra virgin olive oil
- 1 medium yellow onion, chopped
- 2 medium green bell peppers, seeded and chopped
- 1 large stalk of celery, chopped
- 1 teaspoon thyme, dried
- ½ teaspoon smoked paprika
- ¼ teaspoon sea salt
- 4 cups vegetable broth
- 15-ounce can of diced tomatoes, drained
- 2 cups long-grain brown rice or basmati rice
- Pinch cayenne pepper
- Freshly ground black pepper to taste
- 2 green onions, green part only, chopped
- Tabasco sauce (optional)

Directions
Place the dried black-eyed peas in a pot of water and soak overnight. Ensure the water covers the peas. Discard soaking water.

Heat olive oil over medium-high heat in a large pot. Add onion, green bell pepper, and celery. Sauté until vegetables are soft, about 6-8 minutes.

Add thyme, smoked paprika, sea salt, black-eyed peas, and vegetable broth. Bring to a boil, then reduce heat to simmer. Cook until peas are tender but not mushy, about 35-50 minutes. Add diced tomatoes and heat through. Adjust seasoning with black pepper, cayenne, and salt as needed.

While the bean mixture is cooking, cook the rice according to the package instructions. When it is ready, fluff with a fork and set aside.

Divide rice into bowls. Top with black-eyed pea mixture and sprinkle evenly with green onion. Add a dash of Tabasco if desired.

Three Sisters Stew
(American First Nations)

In American First Nations tradition, squash, corn, and beans are known as the "three sisters." Often combined with lean meat, such as rabbit, deer, and buffalo, the "three sisters" remain part of American First Nations' diets today. These traditional ingredients are employed in a unique gardening method that group plants together on individual mounds. The corn creates a post for the beans; the beans return nitrogen to the soil for the corn, and squash leaves provide shade to prevent weed development; hence the name "the three sisters." Corn and beans constitute a complete source of protein, and the three sisters eaten together taste delicious!

Serves 6-8

Ingredients

- 2 tablespoons extra virgin olive oil
- 2 large onions, finely chopped
- 3 cloves garlic, minced
- 1 jalapeño chili, finely chopped
- 2 cups yellow summer squash, small dice
- 2 cups zucchini, small dice
- 2 cups butternut squash, peeled and large dice
- 1 cup green beans, cut into 1-inch pieces
- 1 cup frozen organic whole kernel corn
- 16-ounce can of kidney beans, drained
- 1 quart vegetable broth
- 1 tablespoon dried thyme
- ½ teaspoon salt
- ¼ teaspoon ground black pepper

Directions

Heat oil in a Dutch oven pot over medium heat. Add onion, garlic, jalapeño, and salt. Sauté, stirring occasionally, until onion is tender and just starting to brown, 5-6 minutes.

Stir in the remaining ingredients. Bring to a simmer, then reduce heat to low. Cover pot and cook, stirring occasionally, until squash is tender, about 20 minutes. Taste and adjust seasoning with salt and pepper if needed. Serve warm in bowls.

Teepee Cones
(American First Nations)

Teepees were the homes of nomadic American First Nations living in the Great Plains, which was the broad meadow district on the mainland slope of central North America. Building a teepee was very efficient and typically only took about thirty minutes to set up. A teepee was assembled utilizing various long poles as the frame.

The poles were then fastened together at the top and spread out at the base to make an upside-down cone shape. At that point, the outside was wrapped with a substantial covering made of buffalo hide with a smoke flap for ventilation, which kept the teepee warm in the winter and cool in the summer.

The featured recipe is not a traditional dish but resembles the homes of some American First Nations.

Serves 12

Ingredients

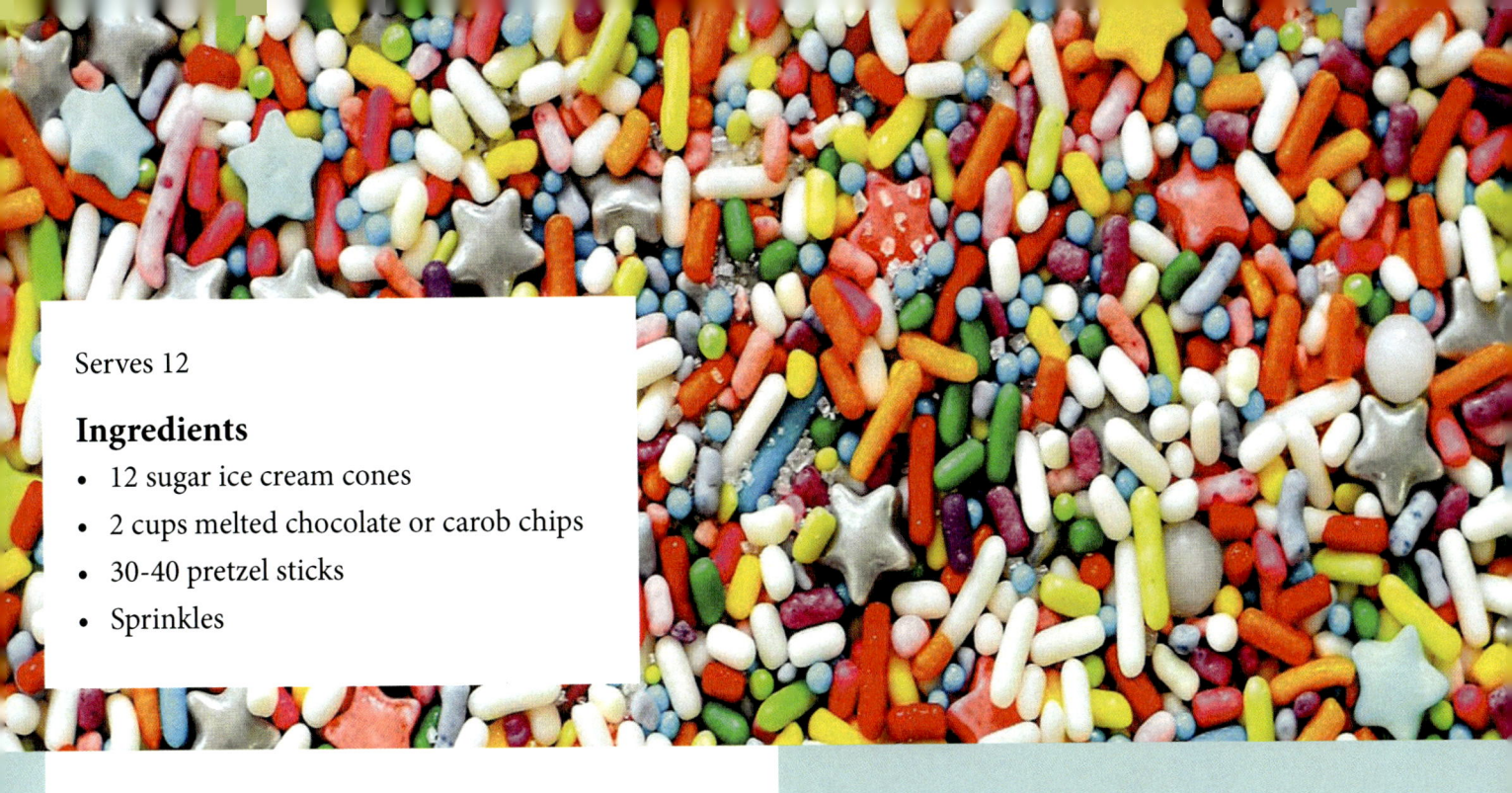

- 12 sugar ice cream cones
- 2 cups melted chocolate or carob chips
- 30-40 pretzel sticks
- Sprinkles

Directions

Cut the tip off the sugar ice cream cone.

Dip the base of cone in melted chocolate. Roll the base of cone in sprinkles. Fill the top of the cone with melted chocolate.

Place 2 to 3 pretzel sticks on top of the cone. Add sprinkles to the top of teepee. Allow time to dry and enjoy!

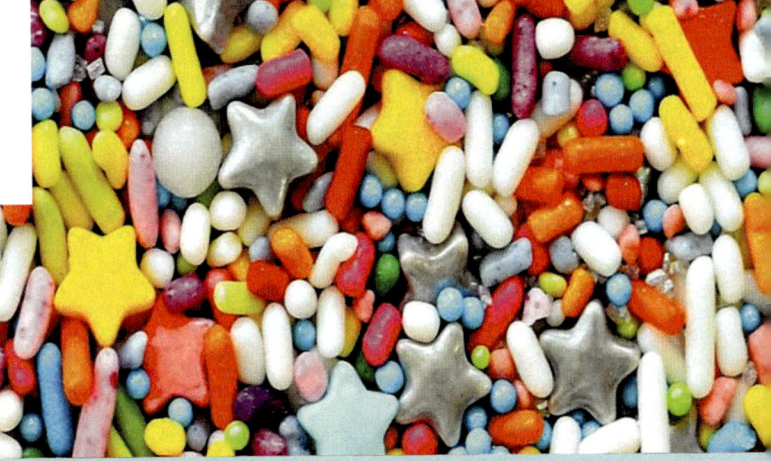

Canjica
(Brazil)

A traditional Brazilian dessert served during winter festivals, Canjica is a porridge made from white maize kernels, coconut milk, sugar, and cinnamon. Known as Canjica in central-southern Brazil and Mugunza in the northern areas, both are derived from the Kongo or Mbundu words for "grain porridge."

Serves 6

Ingredients

- 12 ears of fresh organic white corn
- 1 cup rice milk
- ½ - ¾ cup granulated sugar
- Pinch sea salt
- Powdered cinnamon for garnish

Directions

Using a sharp knife, cut the corn kernels off the cobs. Put the corn and milk in a blender and blend for about 1 minute, until smooth. Pour the mixture through a sieve, pressing down with a spatula to extract all the juice.

Place a large, heavy saucepan over medium heat. Add the corn mixture, sugar, and salt, stirring constantly to dissolve the sugar. Continue stirring, bring to a boil, then reduce heat to a simmer. Continue to cook, stirring constantly, for 1 hour, or until the mixture has thickened to a pudding-like consistency.

Pour into individual serving bowls and sprinkle with cinnamon. Cool to room temperature before serving, or chill, if preferred.

Vegetarian Gumbo
(South Carolina-Gullah)

Along the shorelines of South Carolina and northern Georgia lie islands called "the Sea Islands." Natives of the Sea Islands, known as "the Gullah" and "the Geechee," respectively, share a dish called Gumbo, a popular stew in the southern U.S. It dates back to the early 1800s and traditionally consisted of a seasoned mixture of two or more types of meat and/or seafood, usually in a roux-based sauce or gravy. Gullah/Geechee traditions perfected this dish for the mainstream.

Serves 8

Ingredients

- 1 onion, finely chopped
- 6 cloves garlic, minced
- 2 green bell peppers, chopped
- 8 celery stalks, chopped
- ½ cup extra virgin olive oil
- ½ cup all-purpose flour
- 2 cups vegetable broth
- 14.5-ounce can of diced tomatoes
- 1 eggplant, peeled and chopped
- 6 cups chopped okra
- 15-ounce can of red beans, drained and rinsed
- 2 teaspoons sea salt
- 2 teaspoons dried thyme
- 1 teaspoon dried basil
- 1 teaspoon gumbo *filé powder*
- 1½ teaspoons cayenne pepper
- 1½ teaspoons ground black pepper
- ½ teaspoon paprika
- 1 teaspoon liquid smoke
- 2 bay leaves

Directions

In a large Dutch oven or heavy-bottomed pot, heat ¼ cup of olive oil. Add onion, garlic, green bell pepper, and celery. Sauté until vegetables are soft, about 5 minutes. Transfer vegetable mixture to a large bowl and set aside. Heat the remaining ¼ cup olive oil over medium heat for 30 seconds. Whisk in flour, stirring constantly for 15 minutes until the mixture turns a dark caramel color.

Slowly add the 2 cups of vegetable broth, whisking until the mixture is smooth. Stir in cooked vegetables and all remaining ingredients. Adjust seasonings to taste, if necessary. Cover and simmer for 1 ½ hours, stirring occasionally.

Doce de Abóbora
(Brazil)

Eaten all year round in Brazil, Doce de Abóbora is a traditional dessert made from sweet pumpkin. Sometimes made very firm and chewy like candy and other times soft like a preserve, Doce de Abóbora originated with the Portuguese as a sweet dessert prepared with walnuts or almonds, and when translated, means "sweet pumpkin." Alternatively made with butternut squash, the dessert is very popular during June festivals.

Yields about a pint

Ingredients

- 1 lb. pumpkin or butternut squash, peeled and cut into 1-inch cubes
- 1½ cups granulated sugar
- 5 cloves
- 2 cinnamon sticks

Directions

Rinse pumpkin pieces and place in a large, heavy saucepan on medium heat with an inch of water. Add sugar, cloves, and cinnamon, then cook until the pumpkin is soft.

Mash pumpkin with a fork. Reduce heat to low and continue to cook until the water has evaporated, stirring constantly. The candied pumpkin is ready when it loosens from the bottom of the pan.

Cool and refrigerate until ready to serve.

Wild Rice Cakes
(Canada - The Americas)

Surprisingly, wild rice is not rice at all but a water-grown seed found in the marshlands and waterways from Manitoba along the southern border of Canada and the eastern United States. First Nations peoples, the native descendants of modern-day Canada, fished, hunted, and foraged across North America. Due to the short summer, tribes harvested and dried wild rice in preparation for the long cold winters. As a result, wild rice grew as an essential cash crop for the natives and served as a versatile grain that worked in various recipes. In addition, it is an abundant source of protein, riboflavin, and B vitamins, which promote healthy vision, boost energy and immunity, and prevent many health ailments.

Serves 12

Ingredients

- 1 cup wild rice
- 3 cups water
- ¾ teaspoon salt
- ¾ cup cornmeal
- 1-2 tablespoons vegan butter

Directions

Under cold running water, rinse the wild rice. Drain.

Add water, rice, and salt to a saucepan and bring to a boil. Reduce heat and simmer for 40 minutes.

Whisk while slowly adding the cornmeal, and when the mixture gets too thick to whisk, stir constantly with a wooden spoon or silicone spatula for 3-4 minutes.

Remove from heat.

Shape the rice mixture into patties about 1.5 inches in diameter. Melt butter in a skillet.

Brown on one side (about 5 minutes), then brown on the other side. Drain on paper towels.

Serve hot or at room temperature.

Rellenos de Papa
(Puerto Rico)

Spanish for "stuffed potato" Rellenos de Papa is a classic Puerto Rican fritter, usually stuffed with picadillo, a flavorful minced beef hash, or cheese. Commonly served in many Latin American countries and eaten for breakfast or as a snack, Rellenos de Papa can be coated with raw egg and rolled in cornmeal, corn flour, or breadcrumbs before being fried. Typically a "street food" snack, Rellenos de Papa can be found at roadside food stalls and food kiosks in Piones, Luquillo, and many other places on the island.

Serves 6-8

Ingredients

- 6 large potatoes, peeled and cubed
- ¼ cup sea salt
- 1 cup vegan cheese
- 3 cups vegetable oil for frying
- 2 tablespoons flour
- Sea salt and freshly ground black pepper to taste

Dipping sauce

- ½ cup soy/dairy-free mayonnaise
- ¼ cup ketchup
- Garlic powder to taste

Directions

Add potatoes and salt to a pot. Add enough water to cover the potatoes and cook for 45 minutes or until tender. Drain potatoes well and mash until free of large lumps. Add salt and pepper to taste. Set aside to cool.

To make the dipping sauce, in a small bowl, add the mayonnaise, ketchup, and garlic powder. Stir, combine well, and set aside.

Use a ¼ measuring cup to scoop up the mashed potatoes and form into a ball. Use your finger to make a well in the middle. Place a spoonful of vegan cheese in the middle and close the well. Coat the potato balls with flour.

Heat the vegetable oil. Drop a 1-inch square of bread into pan. If it takes 60 seconds to brown, then the oil is hot enough. Fry potato balls in small batches of 6 until golden brown. Drain on a paper towel and keep warm. Serve with dipping sauce.

Banana Festival Fritters
(Jamaica)

A tropical island with a beautiful climate all year round, bananas are a popular staple food throughout the Caribbean. Banana Fritters, a popular and easily customized snack or breakfast food, are made from ripened bananas that are deep fried with bits of meat, seafood, fruit, vegetables, or other fillings. Celebrating their unique heritage through music, dance, food, and more, most island nations in the Caribbean feature different types of banana fritters during the festival season.

Serves 6-8

Ingredients

- 1 ½ cups mashed overripe bananas
- 3 tablespoons brown sugar
- ¼ teaspoon ground nutmeg
- ¼ teaspoon ground cinnamon
- ½ teaspoon vanilla extract
- Pinch salt
- 1 cup all-purpose flour
- Coconut or vegetable oil for frying
- 1 tablespoon powdered sugar

Directions

In a medium mixing bowl, add the mashed bananas, brown sugar, nutmeg, cinnamon, vanilla extract, and salt. Mix thoroughly with a spoon. Stir flour into mixture.

Heat an inch of oil in a frying pan on high heat.

Use a serving spoon and spoon the batter into the pan.

Fry fritters until crisp and brown on both sides. Remove when done and place the fritters on a paper towel.

Sprinkle with powdered sugar. Serve warm.

Patacones
(Puerto Rico)

Derived from the Spanish word for "toast" and referred to as Patacones and Tostones in the Caribbean Islands and South America, these twice-fried green plantain slices are often served with breakfast, lunch, or dinner as a side dish or an appetizer. Green plantains are a low sugar, starchy food used as an ingredient reflecting a part of Puerto Rican culinary history and culture that dates back to the island's beginnings.

Serves 4

Ingredients

- 4 green plantains
- Coconut or vegetable oil for frying
- Salt

Directions

Peel plantain and cut it width-wise into 3 or 4 pieces.

In frying pan, heat 1 inch of oil on medium heat. Fry plantain pieces on both sides for about 3 minutes or until golden.

Remove pieces from pan and place on a plate. Flatten pieces gently by pressing down with another plate. Return flattened pieces to oil to re-fry for another minute. Transfer to a plate lined with paper towel. Season lightly with salt.

Tamarind Balls
(Jamaica)

Jamaican cuisine is a melting pot mirroring the different cultures that have impacted the island over the years. Despite this, there are ingredients that are unique to Jamaica. From January to March, tamarind trees produce a pod-like fruit that contains an edible pulp that can be used to make an assortment of jams, juices, syrups, ice creams, and other types of sweet desserts. Tamarind balls are made by combining the fruit's sticky flesh with brown sugar and rolling it into round, sweet-and-sour balls.

Serves 4-6

Ingredients

- ½ cup tamarind seeded
- ½ cup brown or granulated sugar
- Sugar for rolling

Directions

Mix tamarind pulp with brown sugar, then roll into ¼-inch smooth balls. Let balls dry out for a few hours. Roll the balls in sugar and store them in an airtight jar for up to 1 week.

Tortillas Panameñas
(Panama)

Breakfast in Panama is normally balanced, healthy, and plentiful. Among all the foods served, corn tortillas (Tortillas Panameñas) are most common to eat. Tortillas Panameñas are made from a corn batter formed into pancakes that are frequently blended with crisp banana or cheese. Panamanian cuisine is a mix of African, Spanish, and American First Nation methods, dishes, and ingredients, reflecting Panama's diverse population. Since Panama is a bridge between two continents, its cuisine features an extensive assortment of tropical fruits, vegetables, and herbs that are employed in the native cooking process.

Serves 4-6

Ingredients

- 1 cup water
- 1 cup *masa harina*
- 1 tablespoon rice flour
- ¼ teaspoon salt
- 1 tablespoon vegan margarine
- 1 pinch of sugar (optional)

Directions

Mix the water, masa harina, rice flour, salt, and sugar (if using) with a spoon.

Roll dough into 4-6 separate balls, then flatten the balls into circles. Make sure there are no creases in the edges and that they are all about ½ inch thick. Put the vegan margarine in pan and heat on medium-high.

Place dough circles on the pan and cook. Flip them every 2 or 3 minutes to cook evenly without burning.

Can be served for breakfast with melted cheese on top or as a noon meal with a hot stew.

Johnny Cakes
(Jamaica - Caribbean Cuisine)

Johnny Cakes exist in a variety of versions across the globe. Modern-day America adapted this staple during the 18th century from the American First Nations as a baked tradition compared to the Caribbean fried delicacy. Originally called "journey cakes" for their ease and durability during long trips, Johnny Cakes are a principal addition eaten during breakfast or lunch and serve as a natural alternative for spicing up Caribbean cuisine.

Serves 12

Ingredients

- 4 cups flour
- 2 teaspoons baking soda
- 1½ teaspoons salt
- 1½ cups cold water
- ½ cup butter or coconut oil
- 1 cup vegetable oil

Directions

Combine flour, baking soda, salt, cold water, and butter in a mixing bowl and stir until dough-like. Add more water as needed.

Knead the dough until well combined.

Pinch and shape into 1½ inch balls.

Flatten into patties.

Heat vegetable oil over medium heat.

Place dough patties in hot oil and leave a little space between each patty.

Fry for about 3 minutes on each side until golden.

Drain oil onto paper towels and enjoy!

Vegetarian Trinidadian Pelau
(Trinidad and Tobago - Caribbean Cuisine)

Trinidadian Pelau likely originated in the French West Indies and was popularized in other Caribbean countries, including Trinidad and Tobago. Pelau shares its origins with jollof rice and rice pilaf dishes from Asia, the Middle East, and Africa. Known as a one-pot stew, traditional Pelau includes meat (usually chicken or beef), rice, pigeon peas, coconut milk, sugar, assorted vegetables, and spices. It is served as a lime (Caribbean slang for get-together) treat and is rich in vitamins A and C, minerals, manganese, magnesium, and phosphorus.

Serves 4-6

Ingredients

- 1½ cups (1 can) pigeon peas
- 1 large carrot, diced
- 2 large ribs celery, diced
- 1 onion, diced
- 4 cloves garlic, minced
- ¼ teaspoon grated ginger
- 2 tomatoes, chopped
- 1 medium green bell pepper, chopped
- 1 medium red bell pepper, chopped
- 4 green onions, sliced
- 4 pimento peppers, diced (optional)
- 2 cups parboiled rice, rinsed thoroughly
- 2 cups coconut milk
- 2 cups water
- 6 sprigs of fresh thyme
- 2 bird's eye peppers (optional)
- 2 tablespoons flat-leaf parsley, chopped
- 2 tablespoons coconut oil
- 4 tablespoons brown sugar
- 2 tablespoons tomato ketchup
- Salt
- Pepper

Directions

Prepare all vegetables. If using fresh or frozen pigeon peas, boil for 15 minutes. If using canned, drain and rinse well with water. Set aside in a bowl. Measure out rice and rinse in a strainer until water runs clear. Set aside in a bowl.

In a large pan or deep pot with a lid on medium high heat, add the coconut oil. After the oil is heated, sprinkle the sugar over the oil, and do not stir. Let the sugar melt until it browns slightly on the edges. Stir the sugar until it begins to melt and look like liquid. The sugar will get frothy and turn a deep amber color (don't go beyond this point or dish will taste burnt). When this happens, immediately add the onions, carrots, celery, peas, and a pinch of salt. Stir around to cook for about 4-5 minutes. Be sure to drain the peas well, as any liquid could splash back on you when added to the hot sugar.

Add garlic and ginger and stir until fragrant. Add tomatoes, ketchup, and a pinch of salt and let cook until tomatoes start to break down, stirring occasionally.

Add the bell pepper, pimento peppers, green onions, and a pinch of salt. Mix well and cook for 2 minutes. Add the rice, stir to combine and cook for 2 minutes. Add the coconut milk and water and mix well.

Add thyme, bird's eye peppers (whole), a pinch of salt and a pinch of pepper, stir, cover, and bring to a boil. Stir, reduce heat to a gentle boil with the lid on, and stir every 5 minutes for about 20-30 minutes or until all liquid is gone. The shorter cooking time will result in rice and vegetables that are tender but not mushy, the longer time will give a mushy or creamy result. Adjust to your preference.

Remove from heat, add parsley, adjust seasoning with salt and pepper, and mix well. Let it cool for a few minutes and enjoy.

Jagacida
(Cape Verde)

Like the Cape Verdeans themselves, Cape Verdean cuisine is a West African/Portuguese mixture. This basic dish, otherwise known as Jagacida or "Jag," is rice and beans, or rice with peas and kidney beans. Jagacida is a staple dish in most Cape Verdean homes and is usually eaten as a full-course dinner with meat or as a side dish. Like some of the best native Cape Verdean cooking, Jagacida recipes have followed oral tradition dating back to the 19th century. Jagacida was originally made with whatever grains were available in Cape Verde, and today, it has continued the same tradition with rice.

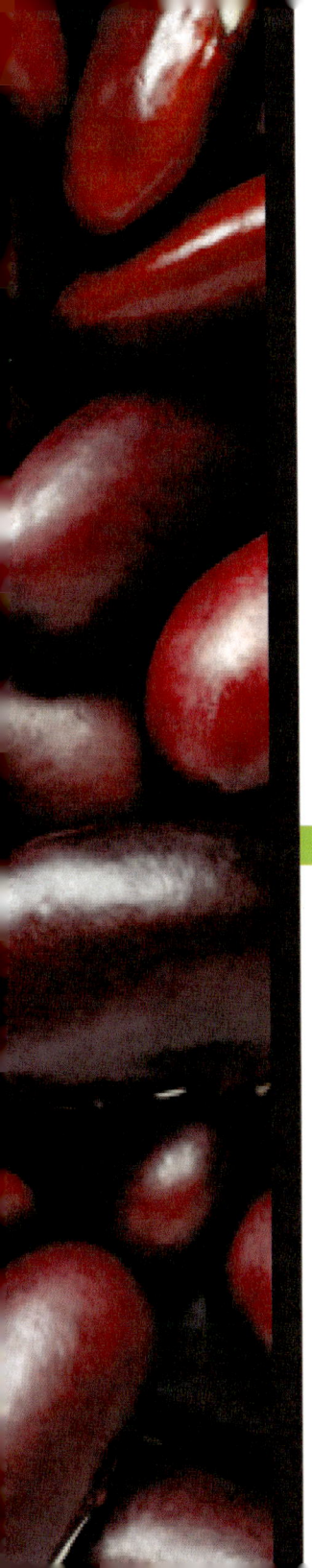

Serves 6-8

Ingredients

- 1 tablespoon extra virgin olive oil
- 1 medium onion, chopped
- 3 cloves garlic, minced
- 3 cups rice
- 6 cups vegetable broth
- ½ teaspoon salt
- ¼ teaspoon ground black pepper
- 2 bay leaves
- ½ cup chopped fresh parsley
- 1 teaspoon paprika
- 15-ounce can of beans drained and rinsed (lima or kidney)

Directions

Heat olive oil in a 2-quart pan over medium heat. Add onion and garlic and sauté until golden brown, 5-6 minutes.

Add vegetable broth, bay leaves, parsley, paprika, salt, and pepper. Bring to a boil, then add rice.

Reduce heat and add beans. Cover pan and simmer for 25 minutes or until water is absorbed and rice is cooked.

Remove from heat and let stand with the lid on for 3 minutes. Taste and adjust seasoning with salt and pepper if needed.

Salady Voankazo
(Madagascar)

Madagascar is an island rich in exotic fruits. Lychees are grown, harvested, and exported from Madagascar. Also exported from Madagascar is the vanilla bean, which produces the pure vanilla extract that brings much flavor to Salady Voankazo. The original dish is a fruit compote made of lychee and vanilla extract. In the culinary world, a "compote" refers to fresh, canned, or dried fruit that has been stewed in a syrup of sugar and other flavorings. It is then cut into chunks and served.

Serves 4-6

Ingredients

- 1 cup fresh pineapple, large dice
- 1 cup cantaloupe, small dice
- 1 cup orange, peeled and thinly sliced
- ½ cup strawberry, sliced
- ½ cup *lychees*, peeled and seeded
- ½ cup sugar
- ½ cup water
- 2 tablespoons lemon juice
- 2 tablespoons pure vanilla extract
- ¼ teaspoon salt

Directions

To a large mixing bowl, add pineapple, cantaloupe, oranges, strawberries, and lychees. Toss lightly to combine.

In a small saucepan, combine sugar, water, lemon juice, and salt. Bring to a boil and boil hard for 1 minute. Remove from heat. Add vanilla extract.

Pour the hot syrup over fruit and chill for 1 hour in the refrigerator.

Samosas
(Mauritius)

Samosas have traveled far and wide, and, like any popular traveler, they have left their footprints along the way. From Egypt to Libya and from Central Asia to India, the stuffed triangle with different names has garnered immense popularity. Generally, samosas are a triangular savory pastry filled with vegetables or meat fried in oil. Mauritian samosas are a popular entrée, appetizer, or snack and can be sampled in markets around the island. They tend to be fried or baked with a savory filling such as spiced potatoes, onions, peas, lentils, macaroni, noodles, cheese, pine nuts, or minced meat.

Serves 6

Ingredients

- 2 packages frozen/refrigerated puff pastry
- 1 large potato, peeled and diced small
- Pinch sea salt
- 1-2 tablespoons extra virgin olive oil
- 1 small onion, finely chopped
- 1 large carrot, small dice
- 1-2 tablespoons freshly grated ginger
- 2 cloves garlic, finely chopped
- 2 tablespoons curry powder (reduce for milder flavor)
- 1 large ripe tomato, finely chopped
- ½ cup frozen peas
- ½ cup organic frozen corn
- 1-2 tablespoons chopped fresh coriander
- Sea salt and freshly ground black pepper to taste
- Flour for dusting surface
- ¼ cup rice milk

Directions

Preheat oven to 375°. Defrost puff pastry until time for use.

Add potato and salt to a small pot with enough water to cover. Bring to a boil and cook potato until tender. Drain.

Heat olive oil in large skillet over medium-high heat. Sauté boiled potato, onion, and carrot until cooked thoroughly. Add ginger, garlic, and sauté for one minute. Add curry powder and stir until mixed.

Add tomato and cook until soft. Add peas, corn, and stir for one minute. Remove from heat and allow to cool. Add coriander, salt, and pepper to taste.

Working with one roll at a time, unroll pastry onto lightly floured surface and cut into three sections.

Take one section of pastry and put the other two under a damp dishcloth to keep from drying out. Take the section you are working with and roll the pastry out until it is about half the original thickness. Cut into four long pieces. Place 1-2 teaspoons of the vegetable filling into the center of each piece of pastry. Fold the pastry carefully over the filling, making sure the filling does not touch the ends of the pastry. Press the edges of the pastry closed and use a fork to seal sides. Repeat with remaining pastry until you have 12 samosas. Follow the steps above with the second package of pastry. Place the samosas onto a baking tray lined with parchment paper, leaving a little space between each. Brush milk onto each samosa. Bake for about 20 minutes or until the samosas are golden brown. Serve warm.

Batido de Piña
(Cuba)

Batido de Piña translated means "pineapple smoothie" in Spanish. A Cuban smoothie is similar to an American smoothie, as all types of island fruits can be blended to create a Cuban smoothie. They are very popular in Miami because of the close influence of the Cuban ex-pat community. With pineapple as the central ingredient, additional fruits can be added, like coconut, papaya, guava, and avocado. Smoothies serve as a healthy treat in many countries with fruit and vegetables as the main ingredients.

Serves 4

Ingredients

- 2 cups rice milk
- 2 cups fresh cut pineapple
- 2 cups ice

Directions

To a blender add milk, pineapple, and ice. Blend until smooth and serve immediately. Garnish with a pineapple slice, if desired.

Sopa de Plátano de Timbiriche
(Cuba)

Cuban cuisine is a combination of American First Nations, Taino, Spanish, African, and Caribbean foods. Some Cuban recipes share flavors and cooking methods with Spanish and African cooking, along with a Caribbean influence to add zest and flavor to the complexity of the nation's culinary tradition. Sopa de Plántano de Timbiriche is a Cuban delicacy made with crushed plantain chips, avocado, and timbiriche, which is an exotic fruit from Mexico. Soup is a regular part of Cuban cuisine and is served alongside main dishes for lunch or dinner.

Serves 4-6

Ingredients

- 2 tablespoons extra virgin olive oil
- 1 small onion, finely chopped
- 2 cloves garlic, minced
- 2 cups crushed plantain chips
- ½ teaspoon sea salt
- ½ teaspoon freshly ground black pepper
- 1 teaspoon ground cumin
- 8 cups vegetable broth
- 1 ripe avocado, sliced
- 2 limes, cut into wedges

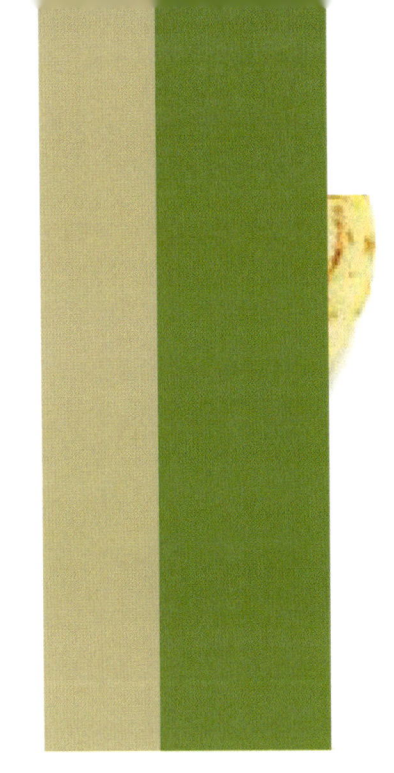

Directions

Heat olive oil in a large pot over medium heat. Sauté onion and garlic together until onion is translucent.

Add crushed plantain chips, sea salt, pepper, and cumin to the pot and stir, combining ingredients. Add vegetable broth and cook soup for about 20 minutes, stirring often until well blended and soup starts to thicken. If a thinner consistency is desired, add water.

Purée the soup mixture in batches until a smooth consistency is achieved (liquid will be hot; be careful when blending).

Pour soup into individual bowls. Add a few slices of avocado with a squeeze of lime.

Curried Lentils with Injera
(Ethiopia)

Ethiopian cuisine usually consists of vegetables with spicy meat dishes. Injera, a type of flatbread made in Ethiopia and several other East African countries, is the national dish of Ethiopia. Served with practically every meal, injera is made with teff flour, a popular African grain, and forms the foundation of many meals. Lentils, one of the most widely consumed legume crops, are a popular component of the Ethiopian diet.

Serves 4-6

Ingredients

- 2 tablespoons extra virgin olive oil
- 1 medium onion, finely chopped
- 2 tablespoons curry powder or *berbere*
- 1 cup brown lentils, rinsed
- 2 14.5-ounce cans diced tomatoes with juice
- 1½ cups of water
- ¼ teaspoon salt
- 4-6 pieces of *injera*

Directions

Heat olive oil in large saucepan or Dutch oven over medium heat. Add onion and cook until soft, about 5 minutes, stirring often. Stir in curry powder or berbere and salt. Cook for 1 minute, stirring constantly.

Add lentils, tomatoes with juice, and water. Season to taste with salt and pepper.

Bring mixture to a boil. Reduce heat, cover, and simmer for 45-50 minutes or until lentils are tender. Taste and adjust seasoning with salt and pepper.

Serve with injera, which can be found at international food markets.

Koshari
(Egypt)

Koshari is the national dish of Egypt. Served in practically every Egyptian restaurant, Egyptian home, and on every Egyptian street corner, this unusual meal mixes lentils, macaroni noodles, and rice into one dish with a hot tomato sauce blended with a unique Middle Eastern flavor of garbanzo beans and fried onions. Koshari is popular among workers and laborers.

Serves 4-6

Ingredients

Sauce
- 1 tablespoon extra virgin olive oil
- 1 cup onion, finely chopped
- 1½ tablespoons garlic, minced
- ½ teaspoon salt
- ½ teaspoon freshly ground black pepper
- ½ teaspoon crushed red pepper
- 2 14.5-ounce cans diced tomatoes (or fresh)

Koshari
- 4 tablespoons extra virgin olive oil
- 3 cups onion, thinly sliced
- ½ cup vermicelli, uncooked, broken into 1-inch pieces
- 5 cups water
- 1¼ cups dried lentils or yellow split peas
- 2½ cups hot, cooked long-grain rice
- 1¾ teaspoons salt

Directions

To prepare sauce, heat 1 tablespoon olive oil in a large saucepan over medium heat. Add chopped onion to a pan and cook for 6-8 minutes or until golden brown, stirring occasionally. Add garlic and cook for 2 minutes. Stir in ½ teaspoon salt, peppers, and tomatoes; cook 10 minutes or until slightly thickened. Transfer tomato mixture to a food processor; process 1 minute or until smooth. Keep warm.

To prepare koshari, heat 4 tablespoons olive oil in a pan over medium heat. Add sliced onion; cook 10-15 minutes or until deep golden brown, stirring frequently. Remove onion with a slotted spoon and place on several layers of paper towels; set aside. Return pan to medium heat. Add uncooked vermicelli; sauté 2 minutes or until golden brown, stirring frequently. Set aside.

Combine 5 cups water and lentils in a medium saucepan; bring to a boil. Cover, reduce heat, and simmer 30 minutes or until lentils are tender. Remove from heat; add browned vermicelli, stirring well to combine. Wrap a clean kitchen towel around lid and cover lentil mixture; let stand for 10 minutes or until vermicelli is tender. Add rice and 1 teaspoon salt to lentil mixture; fluff with a fork. Serve immediately with sauce and onions.

Jollof Rice
(Ghana)

Jollof Rice is a one-pot rice dish, popular in many West African countries. This mouth-watering meal has traveled throughout the region and evolved into several regional varieties, each (one) steeped in the heritage of the place where it is prepared. Nevertheless, it maintains its magic and is relished all over Africa. This dish is most popular amongst Nigerians and Ghanaians.

Serves 4-6

Ingredients

- 2 tablespoons extra virgin olive oil
- 1 teaspoon cumin seeds
- 1 teaspoon curry powder
- 1 onion, finely chopped
- 1-inch piece of ginger, peeled and grated
- 2-3 cloves garlic, minced
- 1-2 green chilies, finely chopped
- 1 carrot, small dice
- 2 large tomatoes, finely chopped
- Pinch of sea salt
- 1 cup rice
- 1 tablespoon tomato paste
- 3 cups vegetable broth
- 1 small package *seitan*, cut into small chunks, about 2 cups (omit to keep recipe gluten free)
- ½ cup each frozen (or fresh) chopped green beans and peas
- ¼ teaspoon ground nutmeg
- Salt to taste
- Coriander or parsley to garnish

Directions

In a medium pot, heat olive oil over medium-high heat. Add cumin seeds, curry powder, onion, ginger, garlic, and chilies. Sauté for 3-4 minutes.

Add carrots, tomatoes, and a pinch of salt and sauté for 1-2 minutes or until tomatoes become slightly soft.

Add rice and tomato paste and sauté for another 2 minutes. Add vegetable broth, cover, and cook until rice is 90% cooked. Add seitan, green beans, and peas. Stir until well combined. Add nutmeg, season with salt to taste, and cook for another 5-6 minutes. Garnish with coriander or parsley and serve hot.

Ghanaian Spinach Stew
(Ghana)

Ghanaians enjoy somewhat simple yet savory food. Most meals are comprised of thick, flavorful stews, complemented by such staple foods as rice, boiled yams, or tomatoes. Combined with spinach, kale, collards, and a variety of spices, and popularly served over rice, yams, or plantains. Ghanaian Spinach Stew is well known in most West African countries and is an essential favorite that captures the flavors of Ghanaian culture.

Serves 4-6

Ingredients

- ⅓ cup extra virgin olive oil
- 1 large onion, finely chopped
- 1-2 small hot peppers, finely chopped
- 2 fresh tomatoes, chopped
- 2 garlic cloves, minced
- 1 cup tomato sauce, plain
- 1 lb. spinach, fresh or 10 oz. spinach, frozen
- 1 teaspoon salt

Directions

Heat oil in a heavy-bottomed pot on medium-low heat. Add onion and salt and cook for about 10 minutes or until slightly golden brown.

Add hot peppers, tomatoes, and garlic. Cook for 5 minutes.

Add tomato sauce and let simmer for 5-10 minutes. Add spinach, breaking it up as it wilts or defrosts. Simmer for 10 minutes.

Serve stew over *African yam,* rice, or plantains.

Chakalaka
(South Africa)

Perhaps born in the townships of South Africa, Chakalaka is a simple, spicy dish of onions, tomatoes, and often beans traditionally served hot or cold with bread, stews, curries, or pap (a smooth maize meal porridge or soft porridge similar to grits or polenta). With tradition or region dictating alternative recipes, Chakalaka may include beans, cabbage, or butternut squash. Simpler variations are made with baked beans, tomatoes, onion, garlic, and curry paste. Chakalaka is enjoyed in many South African homes.

Serves 4-6

Ingredients

- 3 tablespoons extra virgin olive oil
- 2 onions, finely chopped
- 2 green bell peppers, small dice
- 2 hot chili peppers, minced
- 3 garlic cloves, minced
- 1 tablespoon curry powder
- 3 fresh tomatoes, chopped coarsely
- 15-ounce can of baked beans in tomato sauce
- Sea salt and freshly ground black pepper to taste

Directions

Heat olive oil in a large saucepan over medium heat. Add onions, bell peppers, chili peppers, garlic, and curry powder. Sauté, stirring frequently, until onions and peppers are cooked down, about 4-5 minutes.

Stir in the chopped tomatoes and bring to a boil. Remove seeds from chili peppers (leave a few seeds if you prefer spicy), cover with a tight-fitting lid, and simmer for 5 minutes.

Stir in the baked beans, salt, and pepper and stir to heat through. Serve hot or cold.

Atkilt Wot
(Ethiopia)

Ethiopia happens to be home to one of the most vegan-friendly cuisines in the world. Atkilt Wot is a combination of potatoes, cabbage stew, or curry with vegetables and an assortment of spices. This dish is regularly served atop injera, a large sourdough flatbread made from fermented teff flour, and is eaten with the hands, using pieces of injera to pick up bites of food.

Serves 4-6

Ingredients

- ½ cup extra virgin olive oil
- 4 carrots, thinly sliced
- 1 onion, thinly sliced
- 1½ teaspoons sea salt
- ½ teaspoon freshly ground black pepper
- ½ teaspoon ground cumin
- ¼ teaspoon ground turmeric
- ½ head cabbage, shredded
- 5 potatoes, peeled and cut into 1-inch cubes
- 4-6 pieces of injera

Directions

Heat olive oil in a skillet over medium heat. Cook carrots and onion for about 5 minutes.

Stir in salt, pepper, cumin, turmeric, and cabbage.

Cook for 15-20 minutes.

Add potatoes and cover. Reduce heat to medium-low and cook until potatoes are soft, 20-30 minutes.

Serve with injera (Ethiopian bread).

Derere
(Zimbabwe)

Derere, known as okra in North America, is a flowering plant and an essential ingredient in Zimbabwean cuisine. Unlike other African regions that may mix derere with fish or other meats, traditional Zimbabwean Derere is a very simple dish that is economical, quick to prepare, and tends to be completely vegan. Although bread and rice are eaten in some parts of the country, for many Zimbabweans, maize/corn is the staple food and is served with an assortment of fresh vegetables, including derere.

Serves 4-6

Ingredients

- 2 tablespoons extra virgin olive oil
- 1 medium onion, finely chopped
- 1 pound okra, sliced into ½-inch rounds
- 1 large tomato, chopped
- Sea salt and freshly ground black pepper to taste
- 1 tablespoon fresh lemon juice
- ¼ cup water

Directions

Add olive oil to a sauté pan over medium heat. When oil is hot, add chopped onion and a pinch of salt. Sauté until golden brown, about 5 minutes. Add okra to the pan and stir to combine with the onion. Sauté for 1 minute, then add tomatoes. Add a pinch of sea salt, black pepper, and water.

Stir vegetables in pan and cook for 2 additional minutes. Remove from heat and add lemon juice. Adjust seasonings if necessary. If the okra dish is too thick, add a little bit of water until desired consistency is reached.

Nyimo Patties
(Zimbabwe)

Underrated, although well known throughout Africa under different names, the nyimo bean can be harvested green for eating fresh, roasted as a snack, or ground with flat stones to make a kind of peanut butter. This legume is rich in iron and improves soil fertility for neighboring plants. Bambara groundnut, a common name for the nyimo bean in sub-Saharan Africa, may also be boiled, milled, and sieved into a fine flour for preparing a variety of dishes, including dumplings, cakes, and biscuits. Since nyimo beans are hard to find in the United States, black-eyed peas are commonly used as a substitute.

Serves 7

Ingredients

- ½ pound black-eyed peas, cooked
- ½ small onion, chopped
- 1 teaspoon sea salt
- ½ teaspoon freshly ground black pepper
- ½ medium green bell pepper, chopped
- 3 cloves garlic, chopped
- 3 tablespoons coconut or vegetable oil

Directions

Put the black-eyed peas in a bowl. Mash lightly with a potato masher, leaving some unmashed. Do not over mash.

Add the remaining ingredients and mix until evenly combined. Lightly rub your hands with oil. Scoop a bit of the mixture using a tablespoon into your hands. Flatten and shape it into a patty. Repeat until the mixture is finished. You should have 7 patties.

Heat the oil in a pan and add patties. Fry until golden brown on both sides (about 2 minutes per side). Put in a warm place until ready to serve.

Matooke Katogo
(Uganda - African Fare)

Also known as bananas in East Africa, Matooke Katogo is a Ugandan recipe that serves as a traditional dish prepared with beans, rice, and stews. Allegedly originating in the African Great Lakes region, Bantu tribes and many surrounding northeast African nations have relished Matooke as a staple part of their diet. Cooked with its peelings, Matooke is steamed, mashed, and then served. Alternatively, the "Rolex" style, similar to a burrito filled with eggs, tomatoes, veggies, and sauce, is another way to enjoy this delicacy. Brimming with potassium, Matooke Katogo is a healthy accompaniment that prepares the body to absorb other nutrients and control blood pressure.

Serves 4-6

Ingredients

- 7 green bananas
- 3 medium-sized tomatoes, diced
- 1 small onion, diced
- 2 green onions (scallions), diced
- 3 cloves garlic, minced
- 2 teaspoons oil + some for hands
- Salt to taste
- Pepper to taste
- Water
- Sugar (optional)
- Vegan butter, softened or melted

Directions

Place a small amount of oil on your hands before peeling bananas to avoid staining hands. Place peeled bananas in cold water to help prevent oxidation.

Heat the oil in a pan on medium high. Add onion and a small pinch of salt. Cook until translucent.

Add tomatoes and a small pinch of salt. Cook until the tomatoes have broken down and are pasty.

Add garlic and cook for one minute. Cut banana in chunks, add to pan, and mix well. Pour in water until the bananas are just submerged. Season with a pinch of salt and pepper and stir. Cover and bring to a boil.

Boil until bananas are almost tender. Add green onions. Reduce heat and simmer uncovered until bananas are tender. Taste and add 1-2 pinches of sugar if too tart. Add salt and pepper to taste. Remove from heat.

Serve with a light drizzle of softened or melted vegan butter.

ANZAC Biscuits
(Australia)

ANZAC biscuits are sweet biscuits popular in Australia/New Zealand and have long been associated with the Australian and New Zealand Army Corps (ANZAC) that was established during World War I. Made from basic ingredients like rolled oats, sugar, flour, butter, and golden syrup as a binding agent (no eggs), ANZAC biscuits are nutritious and high calorie but also transport well. During the war, these biscuits were used to fundraise for the war efforts at galas and other public events. Today, they are enjoyed by many Australians as a nod to the past.

Yields approximately 20

Ingredients

- 1 cup plain flour, sifted
- 1 cup rolled oats
- 1 cup flaked coconut
- 1 cup brown sugar, firmly packed
- ½ cup vegan butter (Earth Balance Soy Free)
- 2 tablespoons + 1 teaspoon golden syrup
- 1 teaspoon baking soda
- 2 tablespoons boiling water

Directions

Preheat oven to 350°. In a large bowl, combine flour, oats, coconut, and sugar. Melt the butter and golden syrup in a saucepan over low heat. Mix baking soda with boiling water, then add it to the butter and golden syrup.

Pour into the flour mixture and stir until well mixed. Drop by tablespoonfuls onto a greased cookie sheet (allow room for spreading). You should have approximately 20 biscuits (cookies). You may have to bake it in two batches.

Bake until golden brown, about 15 minutes. Cool on a wire rack.

Stir-Fried Bok Choy with Rice Noodles
(China)

Bok choy is a type of Chinese cabbage common in Chinese cuisine. Several variations are grown throughout China, Korea, and neighboring countries and are often added to soups, salads, and other dishes. It can also be steamed, boiled, or, most commonly, stir-fried. Containing an abundance of vitamins C, A, and K, and an excellent source of calcium, magnesium, potassium, manganese, and iron, bok choy is a nutritional powerhouse. With their principal ingredients consisting of rice flour and water, rice noodles are a simple yet nutritious complement to stir-fried bok choy.

Serves 6-8

Ingredients

- 8 ounces wide rice noodles
- 2 tablespoons soy sauce or *coconut aminos*
- 1 tablespoon rice vinegar
- 1 teaspoon brown sugar
- 2 tablespoons water
- 2 tablespoons vegetable oil
- 1 small onion, thinly sliced
- 4 cloves garlic, minced
- 1 tablespoon fresh ginger, minced
- 1 cup snow peas
- 4 bunches of baby bok choy
- 1 small green bell pepper, seeded and sliced
- 2 tablespoons sesame oil
- 1 carrot, thinly sliced

Directions

Cook rice noodles according to the package instructions. Rinse under cold water, drain, and set aside.

Combine soy sauce/coconut aminos, rice vinegar, brown sugar, and water. Set mixture aside. Heat vegetable oil in a large pan or wok over medium-high heat. Stir in onion, garlic, and ginger. Cook for 2-3 minutes or until onion and garlic are soft. Stir in snow peas, bok choy, carrot, and green bell pepper. Cook for 2-3 minutes or until vegetables are tender.

Add noodles and soy sauce or coconut aminos mixture to the pan. Stir to combine until heated through. Sprinkle sesame oil over noodles and serve hot.

Vegetarian Thai Spring Rolls
(Thailand)

Generally, spring rolls describe an expansive assortment of filled, rolled appetizers found in East Asian and Southeast Asian cooking. The type of wrapper, fillings, and cooking methods utilized, in addition to the name, differ considerably within the Asian region, contingent upon the area's culture. Typical Thai cuisine features four main flavors: salty, sweet, sour, and spicy, and meals include several courses. Spring rolls are considered quick, nutritious snacks and can easily be found roadside or in markets around Thailand.

Serves 6-8

Ingredients

- 1-inch piece ginger, grated
- 2 green onions, thinly sliced
- 3 cloves garlic, minced
- ½ to 1 teaspoon cayenne pepper (omit if you prefer very mild spring rolls)
- ½ cup shredded or finely chopped cabbage
- 4-6 shiitake mushrooms, thinly sliced
- 1 tablespoon soy sauce or coconut aminos
- 2 cups bean sprouts
- 2 cups of thin rice noodles
- ½ cup coriander, chopped
- ½ cup Thai basil, chopped
- 2 tablespoons oil, plus more for deep-frying
- 1 package of spring roll wrappers (about 24)

Directions

Cook rice noodles according to the package instructions. Rinse under cold water, drain, and set aside.

Place 2 tablespoons oil in a wok or large frying pan over medium-high heat. Add ginger, green onions, garlic, and cayenne. Stir-fry for about 1 minute.

Add cabbage, mushrooms, coriander, Thai basil, and stir fry. Add soy sauce or coconut aminos, then stir-fry for 1-2 minutes until vegetables have softened. Remove from heat. Add bean sprouts and rice noodles, tossing to mix. Taste mixture. If not flavorful enough, add more soy sauce or coconut aminos. To assemble rolls, see the instructions on the spring roll wrapper package.

Place assembled spring rolls in hot oil using tongs, allowing them to fry for about 1 minute on each side. Spring rolls are done when they turn light to medium golden brown. Place on paper towels to drain.

Banana Pops
(Australia)

Usually made from cow's milk, Banana Pops are a popular summer treat in Australia and throughout the United States. To make this a vegan treat, coconut milk can be used as a replacement. Coined as "nature's non-stop nutritious energy snack," bananas are packed with vitamins B6 and C, along with plenty of potassium, folate, niacin, magnesium, and fiber. Bananas are the top crop in more than 90% of Australia's mainland and can be found in wholesale markets and sold by street vendors. Never wasted, bananas can be used at every stage of ripening.

Serves 6-8

Ingredients

- 2 ripe bananas, mashed
- 13.5 ounce can of coconut milk
- 2 tablespoons shredded coconut

Directions

Place mashed banana into your chosen popsicle mold up to the halfway mark. Freeze for an hour or until set.

Fill the remaining space with coconut milk and sprinkle with the shredded coconut. Insert the sticks. You should have six popsicles.

Freeze overnight. To remove popsicles from molds, run under hot water for 10 seconds.

Note: When bananas are exposed to air or frozen, they eventually turn brown if not quickly eaten. The image on the previous page demonstrates the brown banana in the frozen popsicle.

Sushi Rice Balls
(Japan)

Rice, noodles, and fish are staples of the Japanese diet. Rice, Japan's most important crop, is either boiled or steamed and served at every meal. This grain can be processed into several by-products like flour, vinegar, and bran and is commonly used across the country. The word "sushi" comes from a Japanese word meaning "sour rice." Sushi rice is made from a combination of rice, rice vinegar, salt, and sugar and may contain an assortment of seafood fillings. Rice balls, traditionally known as onigiri, are seasoned in a variety of ways. They are very popular and are served as an inexpensive snack item at restaurants, supermarkets, or street marketplaces.

Serves 1-2

Ingredients

Rice mixture
- ⅔ cup cooked sushi rice
- 3 tablespoons rice vinegar
- 3 tablespoons sugar
- ½ teaspoon salt

Filling
- 1 cucumber, julienned
- 1 carrot, julienned
- 1 avocado, julienned
- Pickled beets (optional)

Dipping sauce
- 2 tablespoons ginger, finely grated
- 2 tablespoons green onion, chopped
- 2 cloves garlic, minced
- 2 teaspoons of sugar
- Juice and zest of 1 lime

Directions

Rinse rice and cook according to package instructions. Mix vinegar, sugar, and salt in a small bowl. Set aside. In a separate bowl, add all ingredients for the dipping sauce. Mix to combine well and set aside.

Once the rice is done, remove from heat and cool. Add vinegar mixture and mix with a spoon.

Wet hands with water. Place rice in one hand, press, and form into a ball. Using your finger, make a well in the middle of the rice ball. Put each filling in the well, one at a time, and close. Reshape into a ball and serve with dipping sauce.

Basmati Rice Pilaf with Apricots
(India)

A lot of traditional Indian cuisine features rice, wheat, pulses, vegetables, and curries. The most well-known variety of northern Indian rice is a long, slender-grained fragrant rice traditionally known as basmati. With dozens of varieties, brown or white basmati rice is a popular basis of Indian cuisine and is easy to cook. Pilaf is a rice dish cooked in a seasoned broth with a mixture of spices for a flavorful treat. Alternatively, the rice may be lightly sautéed in oil before adding the broth.

Serves 4

Ingredients

- ¼ cup dried apricot, chopped
- 2 tablespoons of lemon zest
- 2 cups cold water
- 2 tablespoons vegan butter (Earth Balance Soy Free)
- 1 teaspoon *garam masala*
- 1 medium onion, small dice
- 1¼ teaspoons salt
- 1 cup uncooked basmati rice, lightly rinsed and drained
- Freshly ground black pepper to taste
- ⅓ cup fresh mint, leaves only, roughly chopped

Directions

Place apricot and lemon zest in 2 cups of cold water.

Melt butter in a medium saucepan over medium heat. Add garam masala, stirring until fragrant, about one minute. Add diced onion and ¼ teaspoon of salt. Cook, stirring occasionally, until onion is tender.

Stir in the rice and cook until it begins to brown, about 4 minutes. Stir in the apricot soaking water along with the apricots, lemon zest, and the remaining 1 teaspoon of salt and pepper to taste. Bring to a simmer. Reduce heat to low, and cover the saucepan with a lid.

Cook for 15 minutes, then remove from heat and let sit, covered, for 5 minutes. Remove lid, fluff with a fork, and lightly toss in fresh mint leaves. Transfer to a serving platter.

Vegetarian Mie Goreng
(Indonesia - Asia and Australia)

Mie Goreng, translated "fried noodle," originally evolved from Chinese immigrants who relocated to Indonesia and southeast Asia. Cousin to "Chow Mein," the Chinese fried noodle, the Indonesian version, also known as Bakmi Goreng, incorporates Indonesian spices, sweet soy sauce, fried onions, oil, and sambal, a hot relish made with a choice of veggies or fruit. Universal in Indonesia, Mie Goreng's versatility ranges from street vendors to fancy restaurants and is ordinarily a high-calorie food elevated in carbohydrates and fats but can be easily adjusted to a healthy balance of fat, carbohydrates, and protein.

Serves 6

Ingredients

- 500g vegan egg noodles/ramen noodles
- 3 tablespoons coconut or vegetable oil
- 1 leek, washed thoroughly and cut in ½ inch slices
- 2 cups shredded cabbage
- ¼ cup water
- 1 large tomato, seeded and chopped
- 1 carrot, peeled and shredded
- 4 shallots
- 4 cloves garlic
- Salt

Seasonings

- 3 tablespoons kecap manis (sweet soy sauce) or 3 tablespoons soy sauce/coconut aminos and 2 teaspoons brown sugar, mixed until all sugar dissolves, plus more as needed
- 3 tablespoons soy sauce or coconut aminos, plus more as needed
- 2 tablespoons sambal ulek/oelek (chili sauce: store brought or recipe on next page), plus more as needed
- ½ teaspoon ground white pepper, plus more as needed

Garnish

Bawang goreng (crisp fried shallots; recipe on next page).

Directions

Prepare sambal ulek, bawang goreng, and noodles (see next page). Finely mince the shallots and garlic by hand or in a food processor. Set aside.

In a pan/wok on high, heat the oil. Add the minced shallots and garlic and a pinch of salt and cook until brown, constantly stirring. Immediately add the cabbage and cook for one minute. Add the water and cook for two minutes.

Add the leeks, carrots, and tomatoes and cook for one minute between each.

Add the noodles and mix well with vegetables.

Add seasonings, mix well, and remove from heat. Garnish with bawang goreng.

Serve with additional kecap manis, soy sauce, sambal ulek, white pepper, and bawang goreng to adjust to your taste.

Sambal Ulek

Make as spicy or mild as you like. Any red peppers can be used. For spicy, use all hot peppers, for medium use half hot and half mild pepper (like red bell pepper), for mild, use all mild peppers.

1 cup diced red peppers (hot, mild, or a blend). Salt to taste.

For chunky sauce, use a mortar and pestle to grind the peppers and a pinch of salt together. For a smooth sauce, place the peppers and a pinch of salt in a food processor. Taste and add salt if needed.

Bawang Goreng

- 6 shallots
- 1 tablespoon coconut or vegetable oil
- Salt

Thinly slice shallots. With pan/wok on high, heat one teaspoon of oil. Add ½ of the shallots and a small pinch of salt and cook until dark brown but not burned. Remove from heat and drain on paper towels. Pat with a paper towel to remove excess oil. Set aside. Repeat 2 more times with the rest of the oil and shallots.

Noodles

Follow package directions for cooking noodles, but undercook slightly. Drain, rinse with cold water, and set aside.

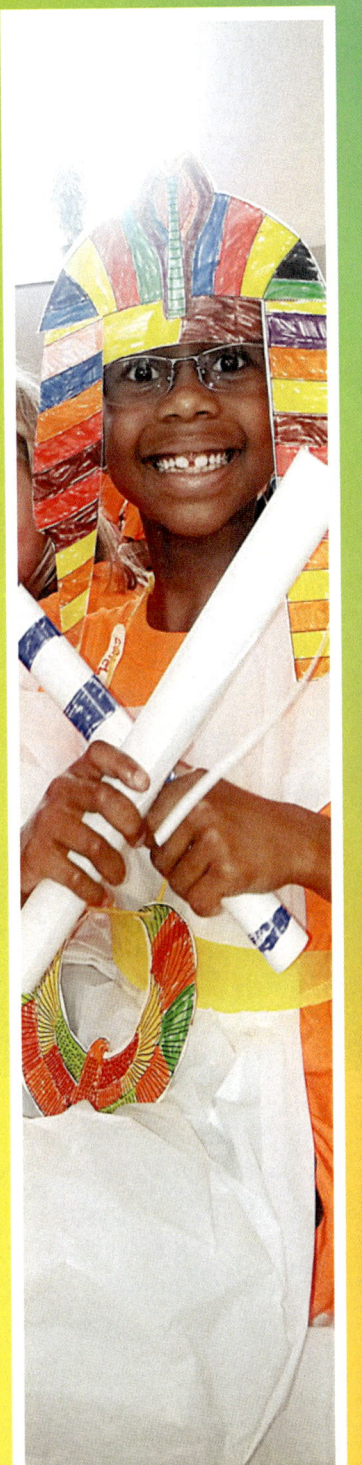

KIDS & CULTURE CAMP

CULTURE

Culturally responsive literacy starts with the premise that world heritage and community are important. Kids & Culture Camp (KCC) strives to bring together a diverse community of individuals that includes campers and staff from a variety of geographic, socioeconomic, cultural, and ethnic backgrounds. In this way, we seek to bridge social, economic, and cultural gaps to build positive relationships and a deep mutual understanding of the world around us. KCC's initiative is to promote an understanding of cultural diversity in a camp environment through value-based education in arts, music, language, cooking, and more.

Each summer, KCC brings together campers from different ethnic backgrounds, underprivileged children whose families would otherwise not be able to afford camp, and campers from communities whose families have not traditionally sent their children to a "cultural" camp to learn about indigenous people. To offset the cost of camp, a select group of campers receive needs-based scholarships which are funded by KCC, private sponsors, and community organizations. Because KCC intentionally seeks out campers from varied backgrounds. The diverse camper population includes children of African, Latin, Asian, and European descent. Parent-educators and staff seek to create a village of love and learning which impacts the lives of each camper and their families. KCC will continue to help campers understand that there is an entire world of customs beyond their own and that understanding them makes a big difference in how they value the world!

Nutrition is another integral part of the KCC experience. KCC provides breakfast and lunch through the Summer Nutrition Program by providing free meals to children who might otherwise go hungry. The program is regulated at the federal level by the U.S. Department of Agriculture (USDA). The Summer Nutrition Program contributes to our campers' health, growth, and development by furnishing them with nutritious meals over the summer months. This initiative allows KCC to further serve the community, and parents appreciate knowing that their child will receive healthy meals while at camp.

EDUCATION

EDUCATION

Kids & Culture Camp is committed to inspiring children to become lifelong learners who are able to problem-solve critically and use their multicultural education as a means to care for and give back to their communities. Campers explore the languages, histories, literature, and geographies of various cultures while dabbling in science, social studies, and math. Yet, some of their most memorable lessons come from the group dynamics of learning about differences together.

Complementary to the academics campers receive at KCC, our instructors promote the importance of character, self-esteem, team building, multicultural values, and openness in an atmosphere that is racially, ethnically, socio-economically, and coeducationally diverse. KCC's instructors strive to make a difference in the lives of our campers as influential role models who are responsible for fun and inspirational academic enrichment.

FIELD TRIPS

FIELD TRIPS

Kids & Culture Camp understands that learning and play complement far beyond the confines of the classroom. With opportunities to take fascinating field trips to nearby attractions and participate in great group activities, there are many places in the nation's capital that are well-suited to mentally and visually stimulate young children. Our campers experience world cultures without ever leaving Washington, D.C. Campers ages 6-12 have enjoyed off-site field trips to the Royal Thai Embassy, Anacostia Community Museum, Botanical Gardens, various Smithsonian Museums, the KID Museum, Rock Creek Park Planetarium, the National Zoo, the Embassy of Haiti, and more! These field trips are often related to the countries and cultures of focus, which helps campers develop and deepen their appreciation for culture and history.

For younger campers ages 3-5, KCC's environment allows for independent exploration and experiential learning through customized presentations. Inspired by our focus on international engagement, special guests have visited KCC from the Japan-America Society, Step Afrika, Casa Italiana Language School, D.C. Casineros, and the Choctaw Nation, just to name a few.

Campers pictured with former ambassador of Haiti, Paul Altidor

SPECIAL ACTIVITIES

SPECIAL ACTIVITIES

Arts and humanities are vital subject areas for Kids & Culture Camp. Many of our special activities stimulate creativity and critical thinking to improve life skills development. Since chess encourages these characteristics, along with strategy, memory, and math, it is an integral part of our program. Exposing campers to song and movement is yet another way to introduce physical cultural expression. Specifically, African drumming is used as a fun way to teach campers rhythm, coordination, attention, and memory.

To encourage healthy eating habits, campers also tend to harvest garden vegetables and fruits for use during our cooking classes or simply to enjoy at home. Additionally, specialty instructors provide classes on money-management and public speaking skills. At the end of each week, campers showcase a portion of what they learned during KCC's Festival Friday celebration through the performance of skits, dramatic plays, songs, call and response chants, and musical renditions. This event is beloved by parents and campers alike. All of these activities have been key to providing a well-rounded and culturally diverse camp experience.

STORYTELLING

STORYTELLING

Fables, folktales, and proverbs are an essential part of Kids & Culture Camp's diverse curriculum. Campers listen to stories, myths, and poems that have been passed down from generation to generation as a way of helping them expand their worldview and learn how literary concepts are expressed in diverse cultures.

Baba-C, D.C's most outstanding, interactive Griot and Master Storyteller, has been an indispensable part of KCC. His uniquely interactive use of stories, rhymes, chants, songs, and narratives support children's development in the areas of cognition, language, social mores, creativity, personality, nature, and their appreciation for beauty in art. Notable children's authors, such as Charisse Carney-Nunes, Michelle Glasby-Millington, and Dr. Joanne Hyppolite, also enlightened campers with their engaging in-person book readings. No wonder storytelling has been a favorite of our campers since KCC's founding in 2010.

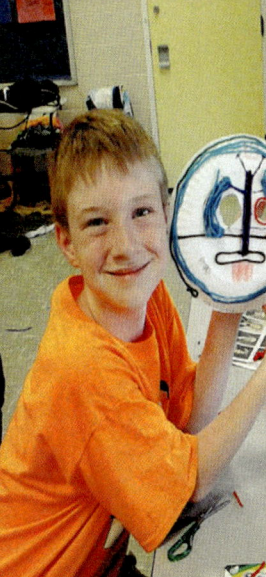

ARTS & CRAFTS

ARTS & CRAFTS

Educational methods and tools that highlight cultural diversity are now more important than ever before. Art, with its ability to promote an understanding and appreciation of various cultures, is a fundamental component of Kids & Culture Camp. Campers explore the art of various cultures and make their own replicas based on the artistic practices of these cultures. Fun projects like clay sculpture, fingerpainting, and watercolor, make art a favorite among many of our campers. Campers also participate in performing arts, using their imagination to present skits, dramatic plays, and puppet shows. These activities engage them in dynamic forms of performance learning while helping to cultivate interpersonal and social skills like improvisation and collaboration.

COOKING CLASSES

COOKING CLASSES

At Kids & Culture Camp, we introduce unfamiliar cultures through the sampling of tasty cuisine. With the expertise of Organic Soul Chef Madea Allen, campers prepare ethnic recipes using flavors from the blended regions and continents of Africa, Asia, Europe, Australia, Latin America, the Caribbean, and more. Introducing culinary arts to children is a great way to celebrate the customs and traditions of various countries. During the cooking classes, campers learn about kitchen safety and develop basic culinary skills under the guidance of Chef Madea as they peel, cut, measure, and mix ingredients. Campers use their five senses, and many are introduced to a variety of fruits, vegetables, grains, and spices for the first time. Sampling traditional dishes from each region of focus is a definite highlight of the week. KCC's young chefs in the making take the recipes home, which allows them to share their favorite dishes with family and friends.

EXERCISE & PHYSICAL FUN

EXERCISE & PHYSICAL FUN

Consistent physical activity in childhood and adolescence is critical for promoting health, well-being, and preventing future adverse health conditions. Research also shows that physical (body) and cognitive (brain) development complement one another; therefore, time spent engaged in physical activity is related not only to a healthier body but also to a healthier mind. For that reason, physical activity is a key element of Kids & Culture Camp's wholesome curriculum, which includes academic development, social development, and physical development.

With soccer as the most widely played sport in over 200 countries around the world, it is our most popular sport at Kids & Culture Camp. Campers also enjoy yoga, free play, basketball, dodgeball, and kickball, among other activities. Our after-camp program includes Capoeira (a Brazilian martial art) and obstacle courses to keep the children active and creatively engaged. Water Wednesdays, our outdoor water play activity, takes the edge off hot summer days and allows campers to just play freely.

INDEX

A

ANZAC Biscuits, 66-67
Appetizers and snacks
    Rellenos de Papa, 24-25
    Samosas, 42-43
    Sushi Rice Balls, 74-75
    Vegetarian Thai Spring Rolls, 70-71
Apricots, Basmati Rice Pilaf with, 76-77
Atkilt Wot, 58-59

B

Baked beans, in Chakalaka, 56-57
Bananas
    Banana Festival, 26-27
    Banana Pops, 72-73
    Matooke Katogo 64-65
    See also Plantains
Basmati Rice Pilaf with Apricots, 76-77
Batido de Piña, 44-45
Beans and legumes See Baked beans; Black-eyed peas; Kidney beans; Lentils; Lima beans; Red beans
Bean sprouts, in Vegetarian Thai Spring Rolls, 70-71
Bell peppers
    Hoppin' John, 10-11
    Vegetarian Gumbo, 18-19
    Vegetarian Trinidadian Pelau, 36-37
    See also Chili peppers
Beverages. See Batido de Piña
Biscuits, ANZAC, 66-67
Black-eyed peas
    Hoppin' John, 10-11
    Nyimo Patties, 62-63
Bok Choy with Rice Noodles, Stir-Fried, 68-69

C

Cabbage in Atkilt Wot, 52-53
    Vegetarian Mie Goreng, 78-80
Canjica, 16-17
Cantaloupe, in Salady Voankazo, 40-41
Carrots, in Atkilt Wot, 58-59
Chakalaka, 56-57
    Vegetarian Mie Goreng, 78-80
    Vegetarian Trinidadian Pelau, 36-37
Cheese, in Rellenos de Papa, 24-25
Chili peppers
    Chakalaka, 56-57
    Ghanaian Spinach Stew, 54-55
    Jollof Rice, 52-53
    Sambal Ulek, 80
    Three Sisters Stew, 12-13
    Vegetarian Trinidadian Pelau, 36-37
Chocolate, in Teepee Cones, 14-15
Coconut
    ANZAC Biscuits, 66-67
    Coconut Milk
    Banana Pops, 64-65
    Vegetarian Trinidadian Pelau, 36-37
Cones, Teepee, 14-15
Corn
    Canjica, 16-17
    Three Sisters Stew, 12-13
    Tortillas Panamonas, 32-33
    Cornmeal
    Wild Rice Cakes, 22-23
Cucumber, in Sushi Rice Balls, 74-75
Curried dishes
    Curried Lentils with Injera, 48-49
    Samosas, 42-43

D

Derere, 60-61
Desserts and treats
    ANZAC Biscuits, 66-67
    Banana Festival, 26-27
    Banana Pops, 72-73
    Canjica, 16-17
    Patacones, 28-29
    Salady Voankazo, 40-41
    Tamarind Balls, 30-31
    Teepee Cones, 16-17
Doce de Abobora, 20-21

E

Eggplant, in Vegetarian Gumbo, 18-19

F

Fruit, in Salady Voankazo, 40-41

G

Garam masala, in Basmati Rice Pilaf with Apricots, 76-77
Ghanaian Spinach Stew, 54-55
Gumbo, Vegetarian, 18-19

H

Hoppin' John, 10-11
Hot peppers.
See Chili peppers

J

Jagacida, 38-39
Jollof Rice, 52-53
Johnny Cakes, 34-35

K
Kidney beans in,
    Jagacida, 38-39
    Three Sisters Stew, 12-13
Koshari, 50-51

L
Lentils
    Curried Lentils with Injera, 48-49
    Koshari, 50-51
Lima beans, in Jagacida, 38-39
Lychees, in Salady Voankazo, 40-41

M
Main dishes
    Curried Lentils with Injera, 48-49
    Ghanaian Spinach Stew, 54-55
    Hoppin' John, 10-11
    Jagacida, 38-39
    Jollof Rice, 52-53
    Koshari, 50-51
    Sopa de Platano de Timbiriche, 46-47
    Stir-Fried Bok Choy with Rice Noodles, 68-69
    Three Sisters Stew, 12-13
    Vegetarian Gumbo, 18-19
    Vegetarian Mie Goreng, 78-80
    Vegetarian Trinidadian Pelau, 36-37
    Matooke Katogo 64-65
    Mie Goreng, Vegetarian, 78-80
Mushrooms, in Vegetarian Thai Spring Rolls, 70-71

N
Noodles in Vegetarian Mie Goreng, 78-80
    Also see Rice Noodles
Nyimo Patties, 62-63

O
Oats, in ANZAC Biscuits, 66-67
Okra
    Derere, 60-61
    Vegetarian Gumbo, 18-19
Oranges, in Salady Voankazo, 40-41

P
Pasta dishes. See Koshari
Patacones, 28-29
Peas
    Samosas, 42-43
    Stir-Fried Bok Choy with Rice Noodles, 68-69
Pigeon Peas
    Vegetarian Trinidadian Pelau, 36-37
Pineapple
    Batido de Piña, 44-45
    Salady Voankazo, 40-41
    Patacones, 28-29
    Sopa de Platano de Timbiriche, 40-41
Potatoes
    Atkilt Wot, 58-59
    Rellenos de Papa, 24-25
    Samosas, 42-43
Puddings. *See* Canjica
Pumpkin butter. *See* Doce de Abobora

R
Red beans, in Vegetarian Gumbo, 18-19
Relish. See Chakalaka
Rellenos de Papa, 24-25
Rice dishes
    Basmati Rice Pilaf with Apricots, 76-77
    Hoppin' John, 10-11
    Jagacida, 38-39
    Jollof Rice, 52-53
    Koshari, 50-51
    Sushi Rice Balls, 74-75
    Vegetarian Trinidadian Pelau, 36-37
    Wild Rice Cakes, 22-23
Rice milk
    Batido de Piña, 44-45
    Canjica, 16-17
Rice noodles, in Vegetarian Thai Spring Rolls, 70-71
Rice Noodles, Stir-Fried Bok Choy with, 68-69

S
Salads
    Salady Voankazo, 40-41
Samosas, 42-43
Sambal Ulek, 80
Seitan, in Jollof Rice, 52-53
Side dishes
    Atkilt Wot, 58-59
    Basmati Rice Pilaf with Apricots, 76-77
    Derere, 60-61
    Hoppin' John, 10-11
    Johnny Cakes, 34-35
    Matooke Katogo, 64-65
    Nyimo Patties, 62-63
    Stir-Fried Bok Choy with Rice Noodles, 68-69
    Wild Rice Cakes, 22-23
Soups
    Sopa de Platano de Timbiriche, 46-47
Spinach Stew, Ghanaian, 48-49
Spring Rolls, Vegetarian Thai, 70-71
Squash
    Doce de Adobora, 20-21
    Three Sisters Stew, 12-13
Stews
    Ghanaian Spinach Stew, 54-55
    Three Sisters Stew, 12-13
    Vegetarian Gumbo, 18-19

Stir-Fried Bok Choy with Rice Noodles, 68–69
Strawberries, in Salady Voankazo, 40–41
Sushi Rice Balls, 74–75

T
Tamarind Balls, 30–31
Teepee Cones, 14–15
Thai Spring Rolls, Vegetarian, 70–71
Three Sisters Stew, 12–13
Tomatoes
    Chakalaka, 56–57
    Curried Lentils with Injera, 48–49
    Ghanaian Spinach Stew, 54–55
    Hoppin' John, 10–11
    Jollof Rice, 46–47
    Matooke Katogo 64–65
    Vegetarian Gumbo, 18–19
    Vegetarian Mie Goreng, 78–80
    Vegetarian Trinidadian Pelau, 36–37
Trinidadian Pelau, Vegetarian, 36–37
Tortillas Panamonas, 32–33

V
Vegetables. *See specific vegetables*
Vegetarian Gumbo, 18–19
Vegetarian Mie Goreng, 78–80
Vegetarian Thai Spring Rolls, 62–63
Vegetarian Trinidadian Pelau, 36–37

W
Wild Rice Cakes, 22–23

Z
Zucchini, in Three Sisters Stew, 12–13

VEGAN GLOSSARY

The following items can be found in most international markets.

African yam: There are over 600 varieties. Many of the crops are grown in Africa. Yams are starchier and drier than American sweet potatoes and should not be confused with them.

Basmati brown rice: This rice is flavorful and has a sweet aroma. It can be found at local farmers' markets, co-ops, and in organic grocery stores.

Berbere: A mixture of numerous spices and herbs used in Ethiopian cuisine. Carefully adjust the amount used because berbere produces a very fragrant, yet spicy dish.

Coconut aminos: Two ingredients make up this condiment: organic coconut tree sap and organic sea salt. It is gluten-free, non-GMO, certified organic, soy-free, MSG-free, kosher, and vegan.

Edamame: Young, green soybeans. You can find them frozen or fresh. Many people know edamame as a tasty appetizer (dunk them in soy sauce … but don't eat the pods!) You can also add them to soups, salads, and stir-fried dishes.

Filé powder: Powdered leaves from the sassafras tree that taste like root-beer. It is a key ingredient in Creole cooking.

Garam masala: Spicy blend of ground spices used extensively in Indian cuisine.

Injera: Spongy flatbread made from fermented teff flour. It is served with practically every Ethiopian meal.

Lentils: Legumes that look like dried split peas. They come in three varieties: brown, green, and red.

Lychees: Edible fruits of the soapberry family. Found in tropical regions of the world.

Masa harina: Traditional flour made from ground corn.

Seitan: Meat substitute made from wheat gluten.

Teff flour: A popular African grain used to make injera.

NUTRITIONAL GLOSSARY

Calcium: A mineral essential for healthy bones and teeth. Vegan foods containing calcium include collard greens and edamame.

Fiber: Complex carbohydrates. Many vegan foods are high in fiber, including apples, artichokes, beans, and pears.

Folk acid: Essential form of vitamin B that helps form red blood cells. Vegan foods containing folic acid include asparagus, beans, broccoli, edamame, lettuce, peas, spinach, and sunflower seeds.

Iron: Necessary for transporting oxygen in the blood and maintaining a healthy immune system. Vegan foods containing iron include black-eyed peas, bulgur wheat, edamame, garbanzo beans, dark leafy green vegetables, lentils, parsley, spinach, and tofu.

Potassium: Regulates fluid retention and assists with kidney function. Vegan foods containing potassium include bananas and potatoes.

Protein: An important cellular component. Vegan foods containing protein include bulgur wheat, edamame, quinoa, and tofu.

Vitamin A: Essential for vision, immune system function, and skin and heart health. Vegan foods containing vitamin A include apricots, broccoli, cantaloupe, carrots, collard greens, kale, mango, papaya, parsley, peas, pumpkin, spinach, sweet potato, and winter squash.

Vitamin C: An antioxidant. Vegan foods containing vitamin C include bell peppers, blackberries, grapefruit, guava, lemons, limes, mangos, oranges, papaya, parsley, raspberries, strawberries, and tomatoes.

Vitamin E: An antioxidant. Vegan foods containing vitamin E include bell pepper and papaya.

Vitamin K: Required for blood coagulation. Vegan foods containing vitamin K include avocado, broccoli, brussels sprouts, cabbage, cauliflower, kale, kiwi, parsley, spinach, and Swiss chard.

Made in the USA
Middletown, DE
14 August 2023